the pin-up art of
ARCHIE DICKENS
VOLUME TWO

AN SQP PRESENTATION

MW01071020

Foreword

It is my pleasure to introduce the pin-up art of Archie Dickens Volume Two. Like the first volume, this book showcases 50, previously unpublished, curvaceous vixens by English artist, Archie Dickens.

Sadly, Archie passed away November 28th, 2004 at the age of 98. He died peacefully in his sleep. Archie was a great artist, a true gentleman & my friend. I know he enjoyed life to the fullest, traveling & painting until the very end. The pin-ups in this collection reflect Archie's marvelous sense of humor, colorful imagination, & joyful spirit. We're lucky to have these clever little pin-up girls to remind us of those traits & to make us smile.

Marianne Ohl Phillips

The Pin-Up Art of Archie Dickens Volume Two
All artwork is copyright © 2005 Marianne Ohl Phillips
The Pin-Up Art of Archie Dickens Volume Two is © 2005
S.Q. Productions Inc.
All rights reserved. Printed in Hong Kong.
Book design by Grassy Knoll Studios.
Publishers: Sal Quartuccio and Bob Keenan
SQP Inc.
PO Box 248 - Columbus, NJ 08022
Send for our free illustrated fantasy art catalog.
Visit our website! www.sqpinc.com

Whose Are These?

English Sailor

Flag Skirt

Olé!

Let's Go Dutch!

Drink Up Pardner!

Indian Head

DICKENS

If Only

Cabana

Beach Ball

Turf In One

Tennis

Wading

DICKENS

Just A Lick!

Kitty

Last Sitting

Bird Watcher

Camera Girl

Bar Belle

Handle With Care

Treasured Chest!

Slave Girl

Just A Minute!

Bridal Veil

The New Aupair

Bewitching

Christmas Party

Carousel

Diver's Delight!

Spring Showers

There's A Delay...

That's Better!

A Gentle Breeze

Still Busy....

Can't Put It Down!

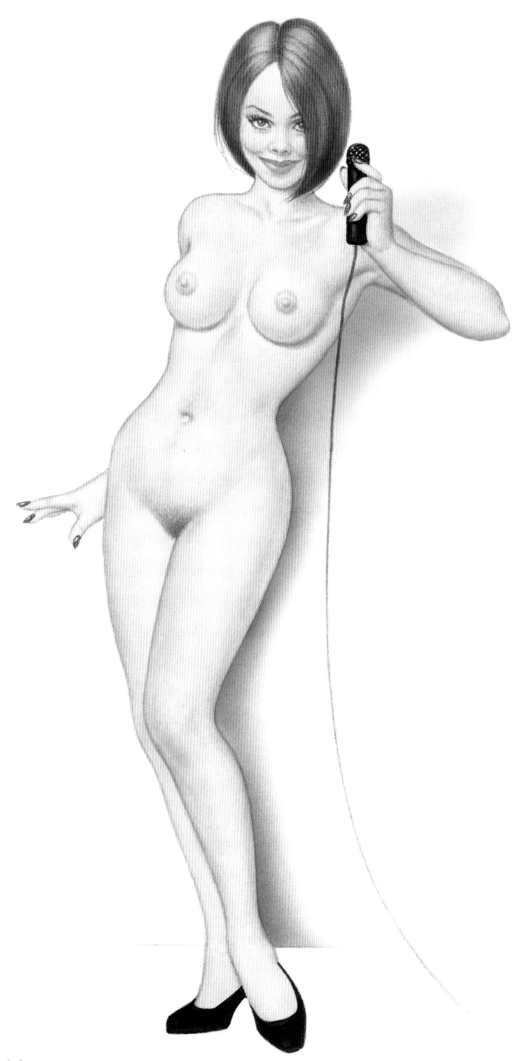

Taking Requests!

Okay, Lesson's Over!

Wish Me Luck

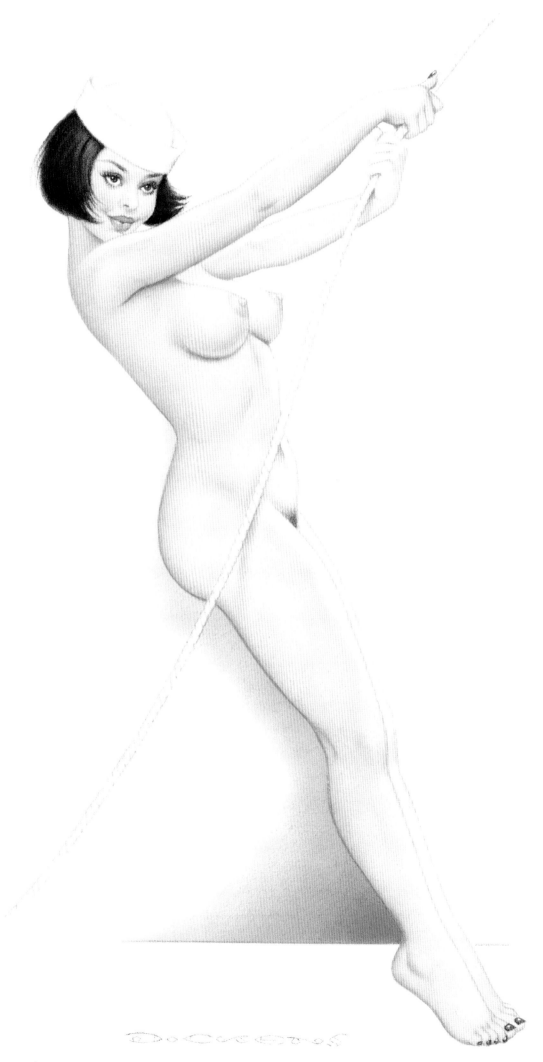

All Hands On Deck!

Howdy!

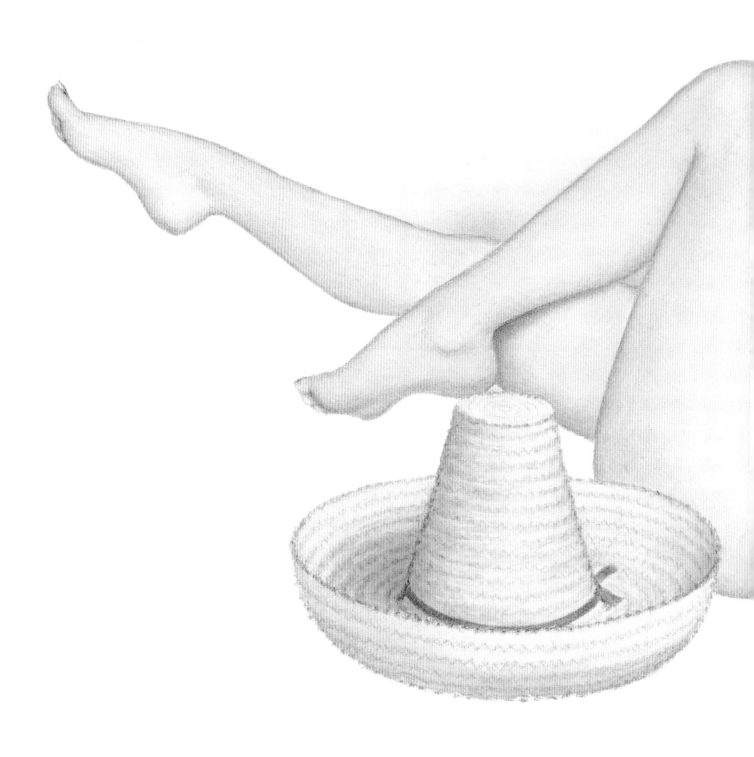

Siesta Fiesta

DICKENS